For all my Little Hippos
—*J.S.*

For Grandma and Grandpa
—*S.P.*

tiger tales
an imprint of ME Media LLC
202 Old Ridgefield Road
Wilton, CT 06897
This edition published in 2001
First published in the United States 1999
by Little Tiger Press
Originally published in Great Britain 1999
by Little Tiger Press, London
Text ©1999 Jonathan Shipton
Illustration ©1999 Sally Percy
ISBN 1-58925-357-4
CIP Data Available
First American paperback edition
Printed in Belgium
1 3 5 7 9 10 8 6 4 2

How to be a
Happy Hippo

by **Jonathan Shipton** · Illustrated by **Sally Percy**

tiger tales

There was something wrong with Horace.
He had everything a small hippo could
possibly need.
    Mountains of food . . .
        lots of things to play with . . .
           and plenty of mud!

But Horace wasn't a happy hippo.
There was something missing from his
life. But he wouldn't tell his sister
what it was. He wouldn't even tell his
mom. And as for his dad...

Well, you would have to catch Horace's
dad first! He always had someone to meet,
or somewhere else to go. So Horace didn't
get to see him much.

Sometimes Horace *heard* his dad.
He even smelled him once in a while.
And if there was a blue moon, he sometimes got a kiss at bedtime.
But all this wasn't enough for a growing hippo.

Horace wanted to learn about crocodiles,

and how to walk along the bottom of rivers
without anyone noticing,

and how to hold his breath.

But, most of all, he just wanted a nice long wallow
with his big round dad!

Poor Horace! He tried very hard to catch his dad.

But he had no luck at all!

Whatever Horace did, Mr. Hippo just wouldn't stop.
There was always someone to see or somewhere to go.
Horace got more and more fed up.

Then, one morning, when Horace
asked him to play, Mr. Hippo surprised
everyone by saying, "Okay!"

"Yippee!" cried Horace, and he gave his
dad a big hug and asked him, "When?"

Mr. Hippo scratched his ear and said,

"Hmm, I think I can manage this afternoon."
Then he rushed off to work.

Horace was so excited he nearly burst!
He spent the morning getting everything ready.
He could hardly wait for his dad to come home.
What a happy hippo Horace was!

He waited and he waited. He waited
until the sun set. He waited until the
first star began to shine. But still there
was no sign of Mr. Hippo.

When Mrs. Hippo came to look for her little son, she didn't have to ask him what was wrong. Poor Horace was so fed up there was only one thing he could do.

He waited until all the big hippos
had gone to bed. Then he tiptoed down
the jungle path in the pouring rain.

Halfway along the path Horace stopped. He drew
a circle in the mud and then he began to dig.

And when the hole was really good and deep,
he scrambled out and carefully covered the top
with sticks and grass and leaves. Then he crept
back home again and fell fast asleep.

The next morning began with a loud
CRASH!
All the hippos rushed out, but Horace
was the quickest.

In fact, he was a little too quick!
Before you could say "Help, Heavy
Hippopotamus!" Horace had fallen
into his own hippo trap, right on
top of his...

big round dad!

    Mr. Hippo looked at Horace,
and Horace looked at Mr. Hippo.
Mr. Hippo rubbed the dirt from
his eyes and snorted . . .

and then he burst out laughing.
He laughed and laughed
and laughed.

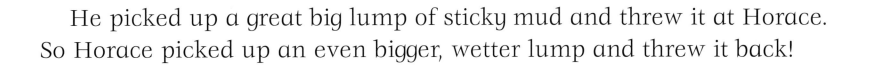

He picked up a great big lump of sticky mud and threw it at Horace.
So Horace picked up an even bigger, wetter lump and threw it back!

It must have been wonderful
mud, because they carried on
all morning. You never heard
such a pair of happy hippos!

After lunch Horace and his dad
rolled on their backs and chatted
about big round hippo things like
underwater bubbles and hairy legs,
and how to walk along riverbeds.

And then they did everything all over again until . . .

the moon rose and the first star came
out. By this time Horace was so tired that
Mr. Hippo had to carry him home to bed.

As he was tucking Horace in, the little hippo opened
one sleepy eye and smiled at his big round dad. "I can't
wait till tomorrow," he whispered.

"Neither can I!" whispered Mr. Hippo back.